MW00396599

This book belongs to:

____

Made in the USA
Columbia, SC
14 December 2020

28148593R00067